WHAT EVERYONE SHOULD KNOW
ABOUT BUYING A NEW HOME

THE OFFICIAL GUIDE TO NEW HOME BUYING

HOW TO BECOME A SATISFIED HOMEBUYER,
AVOID COSTLY MISTAKES, AND STILL GET
WHAT YOU WANT!

THE OFFICIAL GUIDE TO NEW HOME BUYING

Lynda Michaels

Writers Club Press
San Jose New York Lincoln Shanghai

The Official Guide to New Home Buying

Writers Club Press
an imprint of iUniverse.com, Inc.

For information address:
iUniverse.com, Inc.
5220 S 16th, Ste. 200
Lincoln, NE 68512
www.iuniverse.com

ISBN: 0-595-16911-2

Printed in the United States of America

This book is dedicated to my sons, Lee and Jimmy, whose encouragement and belief in me made this book possible. I would also like to stress my love and gratitude to Tammy Festervan for lovingly nurturing this book from conception to completion and to Rhea Chilton for her energy and support.

Contents

Now that the buyer has found a home, the next phase before the buyer goes to contract is to educate the buyer in mortgage finance. The types of finance discussed are; Cash, FHA, VA, and Conventional. Each category is broken down in laymen's terms so that the buyer fully understands the type of financing available to him or her. To assist the buyer further is a list of the most often asked questions and answers on finance. By the time of contract, the buyer has a working knowledge of all finance.

It is time to learn the terms of a contract, negotiations, the presentation of a contract, the typical body of a contract, and other considerations of the buyer in laymen's terms.

Every possible detail in the loan application. The emotional as well as the legal ramifications are documented. The buyer has a descriptive expectation as to what it is like to make loan application and wait for loan approval.

Everything that a buyer would need to know and all of the possibilities that could happen are explained, including the builders responsibility to the buyer before the closing and after the closing.

After the closing, the buyer's duties are picking up his new home keys and making sure that the last minute details have been taken care of. Nothing has been forgotten in meeting the buyer's needs. Every detail is important for the buyer to know, to make the move to the new home uncomplicated.

Construction terminology is an A-Z of construction terms. This chapter teaches the buyer terminology so that the buyer can talk with the builder and understand the progress of his or her home. To familiarize the buyer, is a list of the most often asked questions and answers regarding construction. The questions and answers are complete and detailed.

Mortgage terminology goes beyond finance. Mortgage terminology is an A-Z definition of mortgage terms in the lending industry. It is there to assist the buyer in defining the verbiage used in finance, loan application, and the sales contract.

The conclusion is the overview of the purpose of the book and it's responsibility to the buyer, the builder, the sales person and the Realtor.

Acknowledgments

A special Thank You to all of my home buyers that have made my career a fulfilling experience and to all of my team players in mortgage lending and in new home sales whose efforts and hard work made it easier for me to do my job.

Introdution

"Homeoligist", is the science and study of homes. I have spent the last fifteen years in the field of real estate and mortgage lending. My background and training in residential and new home sales has qualified me to have the designation of "Homeologist". Homeologist is a term manufactured by my deceased husband who has also spent approximately twenty years in the field of real estate and in the lending industry. His professionalism and knowledge has only enhanced my desire to assist home buyers.

In regard to real estate, new home sales is my first love. Being that I love my work, I have spent many hours helping and schooling new home buyers beyond any expectations because I want buyers to understand what they are signing and what they are buying. This is the incentive for my book, "Official Guide to New Home Buying".

This is an easy to read step by step procedure on how to purchase a new home. We will begin with the discovery of the basic needs for moving, the lure of the model home park, the contract, the entire loan process to closing and picking up the keys.

This book was written in an eventful self-explanatory manor in layman's terms. You will experience the buying procedure before stepping out of your present home as well as the full emotional impact of buying a new home.

The knowledge you will gain will give you the confidence and a clear expectation on purchasing a new home in today's housing market. You will learn construction terms, mortgage terms and know what questions to ask before the sale.

Many times I had wished for a book such as this for my customers. How does a sales person, who is personally involved with a customer give the prospective home buyer a class in buying a new home, without sounding one sided? They don't.

All of the talk in the world cannot replace a complete, descriptive, non-bias, factual account and hands on experience that this book provides to the customer.

The Official Guide to New Home Buying will be used by each individual. No two people buy a home for the same reason. You will learn what your real reason(s) for buying is (are) and how to consummate the sale based on your needs for buying.

My goal is that you will visit new homes with confidence and have the expertise to know, to ask and to get what you are looking for in a new home.

Have fun shopping!

Lynda Michaels, Homeologist

Chapter One

The Basis of Buying

"Why do I want to move?" This is the first question that you must ask yourself. It may sound rather silly since the answer is sometimes obvious, but studies have shown that there are twelve basic reasons for buying. The twelve basic reasons for buying are:

FAMILY, FINANCIAL, PRESTIGE, RECREATION, PRIVACY, SEX, LOVE, EGO, CONVENIENCE, INVESTMENT, SECURITY, AND CULTURE.

This is the basis that all sales are made every day. In sales terminology, your buying emotions are called, "Hot Buttons".

We are affected by these buying emotions whether we realize it or not. Television and radio commercials, billboards, magazine advertisements, peer pressures, designer clothing, religions, fitness clubs and all sorts of guilt, needs and wants bombard our minds while we are awake and while we are sleeping. We are a culture of the American Dream and we are constantly striving to have the best for ourselves and our families.

Top-notch companies train their sales people to recognize your reason(s) for buying or to ask critical questions to uncover your reason(s) for buying. All of this may sound rather unnecessary to you, since you think that you know why you are buying and the rest is no one's business. Let's say that you know your reason(s) for buying but one thing for sure, is that before you can be helped in the very best way possible, the sales person must understand your buying needs and emotions. Only then can the sparks of possibilities come together to create an opportunity. Opportunities are lost daily for the buyer and the sales person because of this lack of basic communication.

An example of one of the above categories is Sex. You may be saying to yourself, "no way, there is no way that I would fall into any category listed here, especially sex." For illustration, pretend that you are a single adult and would enjoy living in an area or community where there are other single adults like yourself or where there are a lot of activities for singles close by. Living in this type of environment would give you a greater comfort level of living and a feeling of something in common with your surroundings.

Let's assume that you found the perfect home in a community that was mainly occupied by first time homebuyers with small children. Immediately, some of the appeal for this cute and perfect home would disappear. As a single adult with no children, you probably would not have much of a social life and would have an arduous time meeting other singles like yourself, in this community. Therefore, your reason(s) for buying would be categorized as Sex (meaning to be affiliated with other singles) as well as Recreation (meaning to have a social or physical requirement), because you would want to live where your needs could be met, which is your basic reason for buying a new home.

Another illustration would be Convenience and Family. For instance, you need to live near your work and a day care for the kids. It's vital. All things considered, as long as you have that criteria met, you would be satisfied with a basic home in your price range. Now, you can make a decision based on your needs.

Carefully analyze and go over the twelve basic reasons for buying. Be honest with yourself and begin to write down the reason or reasons for buying, from the list. However, there usually is one reason that stands out more than the others. Take as much time as you need but write down the category and why you are moving beside each category. This exercise will help you and make you think about one of the most important financial decisions that you will ever make. It will be fun and you will gain a better understanding of yourself.

Once you have identified your basic reason(s) for moving we can enter into a new dimension and begin to explore a new phase of new home buying.

As an overview remember that your reason(s) for buying is the catalyst of all new home sales. A skilled sales person will immediately begin to find out what your "Hot Buttons" are upon entering a new home sales office. The reason for this is to assist you and to qualify you as a homebuyer. Otherwise, he or she might as well hand you a brochure and send you on your way to look at the interior decorations.

Most sales people to begin the process, will start by asking you questions such as; "Is this your first time to look at new homes?"; "Is this your first time to visit our community or to visit our new homes? and why are you moving?"

It's important that the professional sales person ask you these questions. Most often people will not confide in or talk with any sales person in the beginning. There is no other way that you can learn about the builder, the product, the qualifications for purchasing and whether or not you even need to be looking in this community for your next home.

Please allow the new home sales person to visit with you so that you both can discover your buying need(s). Just about all sales people have volumes of information that they have accumulated, to have on hand for your convenience. This information includes data on the community, schools, churches, recreation areas, convenience to shopping, hospitals, clinics, bus stops, distance to work and etc. By allowing the sales person to ask questions you will acquire more documentation to benefit you, than you would have thought to question. Without a sincere visit with the sales person, it would be difficult to determine if a neighborhood would be of value to you and would meet you needs and reason(s) for buying a new home.

Remember that assembling your basic reason(s) or "Hot Button(s)" for buying a new home is premier before you decide to look anywhere. Listed below is a worksheet with the twelve reasons for buying and a blank space following each category for you to fill in. Only complete the reason or reasons that apply to you. You must finish this worksheet before going to the next chapter.

BASIS FOR BUYING   REASON TO BUY

FAMILY..

FINANCIAL..

PRESTIGE..

RECREATION...

PRIVACY...

SEX...

LOVE...

EGO..

BASIS FOR BUYING	REASON TO BUY
INVESTMENT..	
SECURITY..	
CONVENIENCE...	
CULTURE..	

Now that you have taken the time to think and to write down what needs have to be met before purchasing a home, you will begin to eliminate builders and locations before you waste your time looking.

Looking at new homes is fun in the beginning. At the time of purchase, you can become so frustrated and so confused that you end up buying a new home based on impulse, stress, confusion and pressure, if you do not assemble your basic needs from the onset.

Don't be mislead by someone else's experiences in purchasing a new home. This is the time to listen to yourself and your basic buying needs. Keep your eye on your target and **keep your needs within your own buying power** and you will find what you are looking for.

Very few people ever live in a home more than five or six years because, in our society our lifestyles can change that quickly. A new home is primarily a good investment for the reason that, it is new construction versus an older home.

Chapter Two

The Model Home Park

You have glanced at the builder's signs and billboards while traveling in your car. On Sunday mornings you have read the elaborate builder ads in the New Home section of the newspaper. The opportune moment has never come into sight to visit a "Model Home Park". However, the time is now. It is now, "The Time", for you to go out and start visiting "Model Home Parks", based upon your need(s) and reason(s) for buying.

Before you leave, carefully check the Model Home Park locations, price ranges, amenities and special offers (if any). With a pencil and pad in hand, make yourself a list of builder or Model Park destinations with the furthest stop first and the last stop closest to home. Dress casual and comfortable. The value of the neighborhoods visited, does not determine your dress code. The appropriate dress attire is what makes you feel comfortable and good about yourself. Take a sack lunch and make it fun. There is an adventure ahead of you, destined to challenge you. P.S. Don't forget a map, and the newspaper ads if needed.

Destination of choice is your first stop. Pulling your car up slowing along the curb with the other cars, your eyes get the first glimpse of what could very well be your next home. Anxiously, your eyes roam and zoom in on all of the magnificent wonders of a perfectly mastered planned community and lifestyle. This is what a Model Home Park should represent upon first glance.

Every bush, shrub, flower and blade of grass is literally in place. The Model Home Park is as clean as Disney Land and has almost the same magical lure and expectation about it. Once inside the model home, you are greeted by a smile and a warm welcome by a hostess or by a salesperson. A natural instinct is to avoid the greeter or sales person because you don't want to be sold or to be given a sales pitch. Immediately remember what you read in the first chapter. This is the "getting to know you and your needs" phase of the visit. It is all a part of buying a new home. Relax. Enjoy the conversation and make notes.

A Model Home certainly doesn't look like any standard home you have ever visited. It's intent is for you to perceive it's maximum family or lifestyle benefit and to fall in love with it. It is a romance with your emotions. It is a courtship that should give you a high and produce lingering thoughts once you leave the home.

Perfection is at its peak in every room and aspect of the home. Is this cheating? No. Is the builder really representing a real life homestyle? The answer is yes and no. If anything, the Model Home is representing the optimum enjoyment of the Model Home that you could ever want. A Model Home should make your imagination soar with possibilities. Is the builder possibly hiding flaws with interior decorating that has been strategically arranged, that I as an innocent consumer would not be able to see? To answer your question, sometimes, yes." Buyer beware. Check it out. In most cases that is not the norm. In simple words, ninety-eight percent of the time, it's called **MARKETING, MARKETING, MARKETING.**

MARKETING, MARKETING, MARKETING, is what a Model Home Park is all about. It is the only "Hands On" experience where the builder can successfully display his homes, amenities and communities to the consumer.

The builder has invested thousands and thousands of dollars in his Model Home Park in hopes that he has been able to exhibit your "Hot Buttons" somewhere along the tour of new homes. Every detail of the Model Home Park has been designed with you in mind. Nothing has been left to chance. Even the color schemes, window coverings, furnishings, floor plans, architectural design, pricing and themes to each home has been a study on current family lifestyles, in as much to what the consumer is looking for and willing to purchase.

The Model Home Park sometimes but not always has two or more furnished homes for you to visit. Each home is unique, different in theme, presentation, furnishings, pricing, design and lifestyle.

As a rule, one of the homes will display samples and selections that the builder is offering as standard features and or upgrades in the homes. **Standard Features** are items that the builder is offering in his homes at no additional cost to you, the buyer. An example would be: color of carpet; formica color; wallpaper selections; vinyl selections; brick selection; paint trim color; tile selection, appliance color and etc. Standard features are, whatever the builder has already designated to be in the cost of the home with no additional cost to the buyer' **Upgrades** are items with additional cost that the builder has not figured into the standard cost of the home. One way or the other, the buyer must pay for the additional cost. These items can range from: 'more expensive carpet, vinyl, brick, wallpaper, formica, tile, appliances, wood trim, enlarged patio, to just about anything that the builder is willing to add to the home.

While visiting a model home, it is very important that you take the time to examine the product brands, warranties, color options available for all of the selections and the quality and type of appliances. Be sure to check the manufacturers of brick, air conditioning, heating units, insulation and in some areas (geographical sections of the United States) it is important to know who manufactures the window units (this is normally useful in areas where double pained windows are standard in the home). Last but not least is the importance of the type and brand of faucets and plumbing fixtures used. Create your own check list of building materials that concern you.

All of the above information should be made available to you if the product is a **standard feature** or **upgrade** in the home. If any product that you desire is not available to you in the selection room ask your sales person if the builder can make them available to you and at what price.

Please underline and score this in your mind, that the price of a home is based on the price of the listed and displayed standard features, building materials, land cost and various internal cost. Extra features means extra pricing and sometimes extra negotiations with the builder.

So when you are comparing pricing between builders, it's also important that you weigh out the difference in each standard feature. That will help you determine what is important to you. It's amazing what you find when you take the time to compare and not curb qualify each builder. While you are still considering selections and contemplating the standard selections or upgrades, the thought may have occurred to you, that not only would you like to upgrade the carpet, but could the builder extend or change a wall in a room for you?

Builders traditionally do not like to make changes. Changes in any structural form usually means a great deal of expense to the builder which means the extra increase in cost could affect an appraisal. There is a whole world of "what if's", "who's going to pay for it," and "can we get the changes approved by various committees?" What might appear to be a small insufficient change to you could be a monumental task for a builder to get approved and accomplished.

Make notes on anything that may concern you as you preview the model homes. After all, these homes were set up to be a complete representation of the builder himself or herself, their style of construction, building standards, and a profile of what the current home buyer is saying what they expect in a home at a particular price.

Now with your notes in hand, you are ready to take your trip back to the sales person who by the way is waiting for you. Take the time, now, to get with the sales person to ask any questions that you might have.

Don't assume anything you've previewed in a model home or model home park. Ask. It is, "romancing the home" and you don't want to end up with a toad instead of a prince.

Chapter Three

The Sales Person

The "Sales person" is literally the key which opens the door to every successful sales transaction. A trained, skilled professional sales person is the secret ingredient that can make your first new home buying experience the, most exciting adventure that you have ever been on.

Stress, long hours and internal and external competition, which is natural in the building industry, makes the sales person become almost superhuman. Sales people are a different breed. They love the challenge of the sale and the continual excitement in the new home industry. Watching customers move in, is such a high, that you totally forget the ordeals that you had to overcome to bring them home. This is true gratification.

The paycheck becomes a reward that one has earned by setting goals and accomplishing them. This is the benchmark of success. Selling homes can be a very satisfying position as well as a very demanding career.

The amount of training, selling skills and professionalism that each sales person has depends upon the hiring policies of each builder. Notwithstanding any amount of training skills, the sales person's only value to the building company is his or her ability to close and sell homes.

Good builders will take care of their star performers because the worst thing that can happen to a builder is to lose his top sales person to his top competition. The value that the builder puts into his people will reflect in the value his people will put into you. After all sales people are the true representation and reflection of the building company for whom they work.

Job descriptions are important. I wanted to give you an idea of some of the responsibilities of a sales person, so that you will have an understanding of his or her position. There is more to it than what meets the eye. The following is a sample of a sales person's duties:

Sell homes;
Follow up on customers;
Keep the sales office neat and professional;
Keep the model in immaculate condition inside and out;
Know the community and surrounding areas;
Have a general knowledge of construction and construction terms;
Put up and maintain all sold and directional signs;
Regularly check all billboards and advertising;
Maintain books on warranty information;
Establish a marketing plan to attract buyers, Realtors and relo companies;
Continually update information on finance and it's availability;
Check on all standing inventory for cleanliness and maintenance;
Track all buyer loans;

Attend all builder, Realtor and community functions; Constantly check on all referrals;

Get visitor registration cards;

Mail out thank you notes to visitors;

Panel homes;

Compute all financial information;

Complete reports;

Establish good relations with the construction department;

Keep a good attitude and build moral with customers, the community and the Realtors.

The list of duties are as endless as the hours that a sale person puts in each and every day. Besides the duties, he or she must always have a clean car, be a good conversationalist and have a keen awareness of every facet of life around them.

The sales person is an encyclopedia of information. At your request he or she will have information on: Floor plans, home prices, known upgrade prices, architectural designs, deed restrictions, schools, churches, day care centers, bus stops, park and ride areas, transportation, fire departments, police stations, medical clinics, hospitals, shopping amenities, taxes, monthly payment charts, total move-in cost, finance, community amenities and surrounding area amenities, utility services, warranties, plat maps, manufacturer information, and any information that would be important and pertain to the area. Each sales person is responsible for gathering their own data.

As I was saying in the beginning, a sales person becomes almost super-human to get a community and model home park ready to create sales. It is incredible the amount of time it takes to make everything look so easy and efficient when visiting a model home park. The side that you see is the fun part. The side that you don't see is the pure physical and mental labor.

There is one thing that I haven't covered and that is, qualifying the buyer. Before any questions are asked or answered, you must take the time and let the sales person determine if you can afford the home(s) in the community.

Qualifying is taking your total debts and new monthly estimated payment and compare it to your gross monthly income, based on predetermined ratios by the lending industry. Ratios, meaning a maximum percentage of gross monthly income that can be applied towards monthly payment and debt. If the monthly payment or debt exceeds the ratios allowed by a lender, then you will either have to look for a less expensive home or pay off some of your debt to qualify for a home loan. Ratios will vary from Conventional, FHA and VA financing. The amount of buying power that you will have will be determined by the current interest rate. I will discuss this topic in another chapter for you to understand fully.

The point here is, that the sales person will know the guidelines and be able to determine your buying power. Once this has been established then you can proceed with your questions on, why you are moving and various questions that you have gathered from previewing the model homes.

Let us now go back to the setting where you are on your way into the office. I will give you a scenario of the events to follow.

With notes in hand, you enter the sales office and are politely greeted by the sales person and asked to fill out a visitor registration card. The visitor registration card is valuable to the builder. The data from the card is normally placed into a computer and analyzed to conclude what the current customer trend is in a home and what the buying is expecting to pay.

In the next phase the sales person would then qualify you on your buying power in that community. Once that has been established, the door is then opened for questions and answers. Don't assume any answer. Ask. Allow the sales person to do their job.

You should now have all the answers to finance, monthly payments, total move-in cost, questions on the builder, community, standard features, upgrades, warranties and all of the questions that you gathered based on your needs.

So be prepared, a good sales person will ask for the sale. After all, that is their job. A conscientious sales person will take you back to the model home and demonstrate its benefits and take you to a planned home site for the home that you are interested in. This is the characteristics of a trained, skilled professional. Expect it. Without even noticing, you will become involved and excited about home ownership. This is the joy in buying a home.

Don't hold back getting involved for fear of being sold. You are getting all of the facts that you need to make a sound decision. We have all heard and read that knowledge is power. It still applies in this case. Gather all the facts that you need. Needless to say, this will most likely be the costliest decision you will ever make. Permit the sales person to do his or her job so that you can get what you want.

Now, with a clear understanding of the functions of a Sales Person you will have a greater respect for his or her position and have more confidence in your judgment.

Chapter Four

The Realtor

The Realtor is someone who for the most part has worked very conscientiously with you showing you resale properties. When it comes to new homes, quite often, you, the prospective home buyer, is not aware that the builder welcomes the Realtors business. Therefore, when you are ready to look at new homes, you take off on your own.

By large, builders respect and welcome Realtors. Realtors contribute to almost half of most builder sales. Builders will request their business by offering the Realtors higher commissions and sometimes bonuses on each new home sold. Then there are builders who will pay the Realtor the same commission as they would make on a resale transaction. Every builder has budgeted it's own commission structure to accommodate their profit margin. Sometimes the bonuses that are paid are on properties that have been on the market for quite some time. It is an incentive to the Realtor to assist the builder in reducing his inventory.

Does the builder offer higher commissions to attract Realtor business? You bet. Is there anything wrong with the builder attracting the Realtors with higher commissions? Absolutely not! Many times a homeowner in the resale market will offer a bonus and a higher commission to a Realtor for selling their home. There is no difference. Will the Realtor take me to visit new homes just to try and make a larger commission? Sometimes yes. Sometimes no. Most Realtor's only interest is, finding for you what you want. Do Realtors need to know much about new home construction to show new homes? No. It is not necessary for the Realtor to be a whiz in construction. That is the purpose of the new home sales person. Will the Realtor attend the closing if the new home sales person does most of the work? Yes, the Realtor will attend the closing and assist you in reading the closing documents. The new home sales person in most circumstances does not attend the closing.

Legally, the Realtor works for whoever pays the Realtor's commission, in almost all cases, it is the seller. In new home sales the builder is the seller. However, there have been times when the buyer has agreed to pay the Realtor a commission so that they could be represented. This is not a common practice in new home sales.

This does not mean that you are not going to be treated fair and square. You are protected by the laws established by your local and national Real Estate Commission. Along with the laws, the Real Estate Commission has provided each Realtor with a promulgated disclosure stating to the buyer and seller who is paying the Realtors commissions in writing. Even though one party is paying the commission, the Realtor is obligated by law to assist both parties honestly and impartially.

By all means if you visit a model home park without your Realtor, please before leaving, communicate to the sales person that you are directly working with a Realtor. Depending upon the guidelines of each building company, your failure to disclose your Realtor could prevent them from receiving a commission.

It is not always necessary for your Realtor to take you to visit a model home park. Sometimes conflicting schedules make it impossible. With this understanding, some builders will allow the Realtor to register you by telephone. If you have a good working relationship with your Realtor and that Realtor has really spent hours with you showing you resale homes, please don't neglect them if you decide to purchase a new home. After all, it was most likely their time spent, showing you the availability in the resale market, that made you decide to start looking at new homes.

By the way, some builders, in trying to capture their share of the market, has placed their homes on the Multiple Listing Service computer in selected real estate offices. Just ask your Realtor and I am sure that he or she will find for you, the right builder in your price range.

There are some Realtors who specialize in selling only new homes. Why? Because a new home is easier to sell than a used home. It is easier to work with a seller with whom a rapport through previous sales has been established—the builder.

New Homes are for the most part in good neighborhoods and good locations. New Homes offers the buyer, the selections that they want as well as better financing (the builder as access to lower interest rates or will contribute towards closing cost). These advantages very often will out weigh a resale at a lower sales price.

A Realtor who is accustomed to working with builders has a deeper comprehension of the construction process and can offer more understanding to weary buyers.

Chapter Five

Learn to Compare, not Confuse

You have made your first run at visiting a new home model park. You were able to obtain facts based on your needs to move, the builder, the community, finance, the home product, the sales person and you have plenty of literature to take home with you. Imagine, you did all of that without saying yes and signing on the dotted line. You will enjoy dusting off your detective skills and touring each builder on your list.

Let me add a word of caution. It is not wise to visit more than three to four builders a day. In fact I would limit it to three builders. Reason. Most builders will have at least six floor plans. Each floor plan will have about three elevations (front architectural design of each home). When you combine six floor plans with three elevations each, times three or four builders, you can have mass confusion. At the end of the day, every builder and community seems to run together and you can't seem to separate any of them. Believe me, I have seen this happen repeatedly.

To avoid frustration, set a limit on the number of builders that you visit each trip out. If possible, take a Polaroid camera to take a few pictures of the community and new home interiors and exteriors. Immediately, when the picture has developed, date it, name it and file it, so you don't forget. At the days end when you have arrived home and are setting comfortably at a table, stack all of your information in a pile. Pull out any information that definitely has no bearing on your decision making and throw it away.

Now get a yellow highlighter pen and a red pen.

With all of your important facts in one pile, begin to separate your piles according to the builder. Take your yellow highlighter pen and begin to go through each builder's stack and highlight only what the builder IS offering compared to what the other builders AREN'T offering. Make sure that all stacks are equal in pricing and etc. For example: "Builder A" is offering a self cleaning oven while "Builder B" and "Builder C" are offering a standard non cleaning oven. So, "Builder A" is highlighted. In the next observation, "Builder A" may not be offering an energy package as efficient as "Builder B" and "Builder C". By doing this, you will be able to make a rational judgment based on your needs. After you have finished this procedure, you will be able to determine, which builder better accommodates your requirements.

Now pick up your red pen and begin to place a plus (meaning a positive feedback on your conclusions) or a minus (meaning a less than positive or negative feedback on your conclusions) in the top right hand corner of the paper representing the builder. Divide the stacks into pluses and minuses. Continue doing this procedure until you have completed your new home stacks. Put them aside for the time being or until you are through looking at new homes and are ready to make a decision.

Once you have finished looking at new homes and have followed the above procedures after each visit, throw away all of your minus stacks. The object of this is to get rid of any negative influences, after you a re certain of your facts. Now, all you have left are the plus stacks. If you have only one plus stack left, then the answer is obvious. Regardless still, if you have one or more plus stacks left, it is time to go back to the model home park and re-visit all of the winning builders remaining on your plus list.

Your second time around will be more difficult. The sales person will remember you and by this time they may have even sent you a "thank you" note or called you.

Make it clear to the sales person that they are in the running for your business and that you are in the process of comparing your final notes. Be sure to keep in mind, exactly what is important only to you. Don't allow the sales person to get off into another world on the differences between the builders that you are comparing. Stay on target. Remind the sales person why you are moving and to compare only what makes a difference to you.

With this in mind, the sales person can and usually is able to go more in debt with your needs. Allow the sales person the floor. Let them run their traps to assist you. Take notes and continue to ask more questions.

A good sales person will shoot to aim right at your target and hopefully to the best of their knowledge hit the bullseye. This is exactly what you are looking for. Straight questions and straight answers.

At end of the day, you should have acquired enough knowledge to form a decision.

Once you have had all of your questions answered, go back through your stack again with your yellow highlighter pen and with your red pen. By this time, you probably already know the answer. You just need to verify it in writing. By seeing the facts in writing, that you have gathered, gives your decision more legitimacy.

You have made a decision based on your individual needs, not hype or pressure. You should feel very good and positive about yourself.

Lets back up a minute and say that perhaps in the beginning, before you were in your decision-making mode, that there was an opportunity to buy the ideal home. it seemed to happen right out of the blue. Before you really got to look, you found a perfect house. It was an opportunity for you to get exactly what you wanted in a new home. Without risking a chance to lose the new find, before you get to look, what do you do?

That's a tough question to answer. I have seen people lose a chance of getting exactly what they wanted in a new home but could not make a decision because they had not looked at everything in the market.

For your sake, let me say this. If a home fits all of your needs and is exactly what you are looking for in a new home, sometimes it is just not necessary to look any further. Under these circumstances, I would ask the sales person if I could put a deposit on the property to hold it over night.

Go home and weigh out all the pros and cons with your yellow high-lighter pen and red pen if necessary. Don't be afraid to trust your instincts. The next morning go back out to the home, walk in it, sit in it talk in it and mentally arrange your furniture. In fact I would advise the above step before you make your final decision on any home. If you still feel the same way and are excited about the new home, then go for it. Write up a con-tract and get the home off the market.

Occasionally this happens. When given the right opportunity to place a deposit and weigh out the pros and the cons, the buyer is delighted. Fortunately, the buyer did not have to search and wait to find what they wanted. The thrill and joy of buying a home is the same, because what really counts is that you get what you want.

Chapter Six

Finance

Before we go back to the sales office and write the contract, lets preview the financing options.

For a moment, lets assume that you were given financing information from each builder that you interviewed. It is a common practice for builders to acquire the best possible financing available on the market. The reason is simple. Excellent financing sells houses.

The builders access to reaching the lenders is greater than yours to strike a deal. By a deal, I mean, the builder's ability to purchase a commitment on money. A commitment is, the lenders promise to lend money at a specific interest rate to a or at a specified date in the future at a determined cost to the builder by the lender. What the builder pays to obtain the commitment money is confidential between the builder and the lender. The good side of it is, that you can get an excellent interest rate usually at no additional cost to you and the lower interest rate allows you, the buyer to purchase more house for the money.

As I stated earlier, if you have interviewed each builder properly, the sales person has qualified you based upon the best financing that was available to the builder or in the market.

Okay, now lets go over the different types of loans and cover their guidelines and describe it in layman's terms. There are five ways that a home can be bought or financed and they are; cash, FHA, VA, Conventional, and outside financing.

CASH; Cash is a simple transaction. On a cash sale, the builder will often offer a cash discount because he is not having to pay points and other closing cost as he would in a financed sale. The amount of the discount varies. It all depends upon the builders bottom line, after all, his profit margin is the same regardless if it's a cash or financed sale.

In a cash sale, the buyer will take to the closing a certified check for the agreed sale amount plus their minimal closing cost. The closing cost will vary from city to city but since there is no mortgage, the cost should be; the attorney fee charges, survey, document and recording fee charges and any other charges required by your state. Remember, that you only pay your vested interest of charges to actually pass title into your name. There is no mortgage company to set up any requirements for closing cost and or escrow accounts.

FHA LOAN; FHA is the FEDERAL HOUSING ADMINISTRA-TION, a government agency established in 1934. It was assimilated into the DEPARTMENT OF HOUSING AND URBAN DEVELOPMENT (HUD) in November, 1965. Its basic purpose was to make home owner-ship a possibility for all financially qualified people.

FHA's original objectives were to exert a stabilizing influence on mort-gage loan interest rates. To minimize down payment requirements and to establish a level payment amortization for home loans. FHA also was to provide a vehicle whereby institutional investors would be attracted to invest in residential mortgage loans. The basic function of FHA today is still very much aligned with its original objectives. The general function of FHA is to insure mortgage lenders against loss in the event of foreclosure on any property covered by an FHA loan.

FHA maximum loan limits are different in every region of the United States (maximum loan limits can change). There are Builders who build within these maximum loan limits. Before a builder can offer FHA financing on any of his homes, he has to be FHA approved. In other words, FHA has to approve all of his plans and specifications on each home according to FHA guidelines before he can offer FHA financing. An FHA inspector from FHA has to inspect and pass all of his homes before a buyer can close on a house. Not only does the house have to be approved, inspected and passed by FHA but it also has to have an FHA appraisal before a buyer can close on a house.

Not to worry, a builder who is building according to FHA guidelines knows the rules and is prepared for FHA.

The basic FHA program use by borrowers is the FHA 203B. The characteristics of the 203B loan are: the principal and interest payments remain fixed over the life of the loan; the down payment is minimal; there is no negative amortization and the loan is available to anyone who qualifies.

To qualify (as of this writing) FHA requires that your total monthly housing expense (including principal, interest, insurance, taxes, maintenance and or homeowner's association fees) does not exceed 29% of your gross monthly income. You do this by taking your total housing expense divided by your gross monthly income. This percentage should not exceed 29%. Next, take your total monthly housing expense, child support (if any), student loans (if any), all revolving accounts, notes and installment notes which extend over 12 months such as a car loan, boat loans, co-signer notes, etc. and charge card minimum monthly payments. If you have charge cards that are not in use, FHA requires that you add $ 1 0 to your debt for every unused charge card. The charge card account has to have been closed for at least one year before they will not count the card as a debt. Take your total monthly debt (as described above) and divide that amount by your gross monthly income. This amount should not exceed 41%.

Mortgage Insurance is required on all FHA loans regardless of the loan to value ratio. The amount of your down payment has no effect determining if Mortgage Insurance is necessary (unlike Conventional loans). Mortgage Insurance is the consideration paid on all FHA loans by the borrower in the amount of 3.8% (this amount varies depending upon the down payment) of the loan amount. It can be financed into the loan amount or paid in cash at closing. FHA can insure the loan because the buyer is required to pay for the insurance premium.

FHA guidelines and ratios can change. Ask your sales person what the current FHA ratios (percentages) are today. Qualifying yourself ahead of time will give you an adequate idea of what you can be approved for and purchase according to FHA guidelines.

FHA allows the borrower to move into a home with lower closing cost and a lower down payment. It is a great loan, because it doesn't require a lot of money to get into a home.

VA **LOAN**; VETERANS ADMINISTRATION guarantees loans on residences for veteran purchasers. These loans are attractive to mortgage loan investors since the guarantee acts as a protection to the investor.

The Veterans Administration is a government agency established in 1930. Its primary function is to help those who have served their country in the armed forces, as well as any surviving family members. The Veterans Administration's programs have offered a very viable type of financing for veterans across the country.

Basically, the government mandates a VA loan interest rate ceiling. The veteran must be an owner occupant. There is no required cost to the veteran for the guaranty of a mortgage loan. VA permits 100% loans and they can be assumed with no escalation of interest rate and no qualification of the new borrower. A co-borrower must be a legal spouse or another veteran on the original loan.

Eligible borrowers are veterans who have been discharged under other than dishonorable conditions, active duty veterans who have completed 181 days of active duty, a veteran discharged for hardship or disability, a surviving spouse of a veteran who has not remarried, spouses of members of the armed forces on active duty who have been listed for more than 90 days as missing in action, captured in the line of duty by a hostile force, or forcibly detained by a foreign government or power.

To determine that a veteran is eligible for a VA loan, a Certificate of Eligibility must be obtained. This is done by submitting to VA a form along with the veteran's DD-214 (discharge paper or separation Certificate). The DD-214 form indicates the date entered and separated from military duty, type of discharge, and any time lost during service. If the veteran is currently on active duty, then any prior DD-214 forms and a statement from the commanding officer are needed.

A Certificate of Eligibility, when issued to a veteran while on active duty, is "valid unless discharged or released subsequent to date of this certificate." A certification of continuous active duty as of the date execution of the note is required.

Ineligible borrowers are veterans with other than Honorable Discharge and Reservist.

The term "guaranty" means the obligation of the United States to repay a specific percentage of a loan upon the default of the primary borrower. The maximum guaranty that is given on any one loan made by VA to an eligible veteran may not exceed 60% of the loan amount or currently $27,500 whichever is less.

Entitlement means the guaranty or insurance benefit available to an eligible veteran. A veteran is eligible for a VA loan as long as he has entitlement remaining.

If a veteran has a VA loan and wishes to restore his or her entitlement, it can be restored under the following circumstances; The veteran must sell his or her VA home loan under new financing so that his or her entitlement can be reinstated for the full amount; or the veteran can transfer entitlement from one veteran to another eligible veteran purchaser by the substitution of entitlement.

A veteran can obtain a 100% loan for a period of 30 years. Most lenders will lend up to $1 10,000 with no required down payment. Some lenders have raised the maximum loan to $144,000 with a 25% down payment required on the amount in excess of $1 1 0, 000. Check in your area with a VA lender.

The VA uses the ratio method for qualifying veterans for mortgage loans. The qualifying ratio of 41% is based on total monthly obligations (housing expense, recurring debts, and job related expenses) to gross monthly income.

Housing expense includes payments to principal and interest, real estate taxes, hazard insurance and homeowners association dues.

Recurring debts are debts which extend over a 6 month period including a minimum payment for revolving accounts which have no balance but have been used during the last year.

The formula for qualifying is; Total housing expense plus Recurring Debts divided by Gross monthly income. This ratio or percentage should not exceed 41%.

VA does require a Certificate of Reasonable Value (CRV) on all homes closed by VA. The CRV is issued by VA after it has received the appraisal report from the fee appraiser.

A funding fee of 2.25% (this amount could vary) of the loan amount will be collected by VA. The veteran or the selling party may pay the funding fee in cash at the time of closing or it may be financed in the loan amount.

Even though the veteran is not required to put down a down payment, the veteran will still be responsible in most cases for some closing cost as determined by the builders contract. For example; the veteran is responsible for obtaining hazard insurance, the required amount of taxes in an escrow account, some attorney fees, miscellaneous closing fees and most builders prefer that the veteran pay their own VA funding fee. However, I am not setting up any standards as to what the veteran is required to pay. That is up to the builder and what he can afford to pay, in order to sell a home on a VA loan. A VA loan cost the builder more money than any other type of financing.

If a veteran is interested in using their VA benefits to buy a new home, first check with VA on the amount of eligibility available and then check with each builder's sales person as to the total move-in cost required by each builder.

CONVENTIONAL LOANS; Conventional loans are residential loans which are not insured by FHA or guaranteed by the Veterans Administration. These loans typically require the borrower to make a minimum down payment of 5%. Private Mortgage Insurance is required by the lender or investor if the down payment is less than 20%. Conventional loans are separated into two categories. They are Conforming and Non Conforming.

Conforming Conventional loans have loan to value ratios and maximum loan amounts which fall within FNMA (Fannie Mae) and FHLMC (Freddie Mac) established guidelines. These loans are acceptable for purchase by FNMA and FHLMC.

Maximum loan amounts and loan to value ratios will vary from region to region.

Non Conforming Conventional loans exceed the maximum loan amounts or loan to value ratios of conforming conventional loans. Non Conforming loans are either sold to private investors or retained in the portfolio of the mortgage lender. The maximum acceptable loan amounts and loan to value ratios are determined by each investor.

Mortgage Insurance (MI) is the guaranty of a private underwriting company which insures a mortgage lender or his investors against losses due to foreclosure. For a MI company to insure a mortgage loan, they collect insurance premiums based upon the loan-to-value ratio and the type of loan.

Standards for private Mortgage Insurance companies are approved in each state by the state Insurance Commissioner so the rates may differ from state to state.

Standard conventional underwriting sets maximum ratios that a borrower's income compared to the new mortgage payment and his or her other debt payments must meet.

The total monthly house payment (including principal, interest, taxes, hazard insurance, and PMI, if applicable) should not exceed 33% of the monthly gross income. To arrive at this ratio (percentage), divide the total monthly house payment by the monthly gross income. Now take the total monthly house payment plus any other monthly debts and add them together. Divide that number by the monthly gross income. The total debt should not exceed 38% of the monthly gross income.

These maximum qualifying ratios are guidelines for prudent lending. As guidelines, they are not cast in stone. It is up to the lender to determine the buyers qualifications on ratios.

OUTSIDE FINANCING; Is any other source of financing not mentioned above that the builder agrees upon the terms and conditions.

DISCOUNT POINT; A Discount Point is the up front money that a lender makes on a loan. When the laws changed and did away with the prepayment penalty on all loans, lenders lost their ability to get a better yield on their loans. The result was the discount point system.

A discount point is 1% of the loan amount. The lender has to have a required yield on a loan. The lower the interest rate the higher the discount points. The higher the interest rate the lower the discount points. The discount points are the cost paid to buy down an interest rate.

In most cases the builder either pays all or part of the points.

THE APPRAISAL; The purpose of the appraisal is to determine the maximum mortgage amount by the lender. The lender can not lend more money than the home is valued for.

Appraisals can be complex or simple depending upon whose doing the appraisal. FHA, VA and Conventional appraisals are all determined by their own set of rules. It is very important that the appraisal come in around the sales price of the home, so that you, the borrower and the builder can successful complete the sale of the home.

VA and FHA can change the rules in the middle of the game. For you to stay completely updated, I urge you to contact an FHA or VA approved lender to verify any question that you might have. The same applies to checking loan limits. Loan limits can vary considerably from region to region within a state.

To extend what we have just covered in this chapter, listed below are the most frequent asked questions regarding finance.

Q: Who is eligible for an FHA loan?
A: Anyone that can qualify under the credit guidelines. They must be a citizen or have obtained permanent residence status (green card) in the U.S.A.

Q: What is FHA insurance?
A: This is the insurance by the FHA to a private lender that in the event of default by the mortgagor, the balance of the loan will be repaid.

Q: When does the buyer pay FHA mortgage insurance?
A: Either in a lump sum at closing or financed as part of the loan amount.

Q: What is the maximum loan insured by FHA?
A: This is a regional requirement set by FHA, every region of the U.S. varies.

Q: Does FHA loan money to home buyers?

A: No. It only insures the loan made to qualified mortgagors by private lenders.

Q: What is the most common FHA financing program.

A: 203B—a 30 year fixed rate.

Q: What are the FHA commitments?

A: There are two types if commitments: Conditional Commitment-Appraisal of property value, closing cost and explanation date on a particular piece of property. The second commitment is Firm Commitment—Loan approval stating conditions, if required for closing.

Q: What items does a loan company require in order to submit a loan to FHA for approval?

A: Section 203B: FHA conditional commitment, Two year employment coverage, Copy of sales contract, Verification of money needed to close, Credit report and other pertinent data, Signed form 2900 (application for mortgagor approval and firm commitment.

Q: How long does it take to get a loan approved FHA?

A: Four to eight weeks. It depends on the circumstances of each individual case.

Q: Can you charge more for a house than a FHA conditional commitment amount?

A: Yes. You may charge more than the value of the FHA commitment provided that the buyer has been informed of the extra amount being charged and he agreed to pay the extra amount with non borrowed money at closing.

Q: What are closing cost?

A: Closing cost are all involved in rendering a lien free title that is acceptable to the FHA and the lending institution.

Q: What are FHA prepaid items?

A: 14 months of homeowner's insurance, 3 to 4 months taxes and pre-liminary interest from the date of closing to the end of the month or funding date.

Q: Can you give anything away under FHA?

A: No.

Q: Does it matter if the current applicant has had a prior FHA loan?

A: Yes. If someone has sold a home financed by an FHA loan in the last two years (on an assumption), the previously owned   Property must have at least 15% equity into it to obtain a 5% or less down payment on the new FHA home loan. The previous property, has to establish it's value by an independent appraisal, paid for by the buyer who is obtaining the new home loan. If the appraisal shows that the property does not have a 15% equity into it, then the buyer must put down a down payment of 15% or more into the new FHA home loan. On the other hand, if the appraisal shows that the property has 15% or more equity into it, the buyer is then allowed to put down a 5% or less down payment on the new home loan. If the buyer has an existing FHA home loan on property that the buyer is or will be renting, then the buyer has to put down a minimum down payment of 25% on the new FHA home loan.

Q: Can an FHA loan be paid off without a penalty?

A: Yes.

Q: Can a Conventional home ever be sold FHA?
A: Yes. A conventional home loan can be sold FHA if it can pass conformance inspection.

Q: What is a VA loan?
A: A government insured loan for veterans.

Q: What is a VA loan guaranty?
A: It is the obligation of the United States to repay a specific percentage of a loan upon the default of the primary debtor.

Q: How much loan guaranty is a veteran eligible for?
A: $27,500 (called his\her entitlement).

Q: What is a certificate of eligibility.
A: It is a certificate issued by the Veterans Administration that indicates the eligibility of the veteran for a VA loan guaranty.

Q: Are World War 11 veterans still eligible?
A: Yes, as long as the veteran has entitlement.

Q: What is the maximum VA loan?
A: $1 10,000. Some lenders have a maximum loan amount of $144,000, depending on region.

Q: What is the maximum term of a VA loan?
A: 30 years.

Q: What is a CRV?
A: A Certificate of Reasonable Value is a VA appraisal on proposed or existing piece of property.

Q: What items does a loan company need before submitting a VA loan for approval?

A: Certificate of Reasonable Value, Certificate of Eligibility, Two year employment coverage, Credit report, Bank verification, and any other pertinent information needed to get a loan approved.

Q: How long does it take to get a VA loan approved?

A: Six to ten weeks, depending upon the individual.

Q: Is a veteran responsible for complete payment on his loan?

A: Yes.

Q: Can a loan be obtained for a veteran who has used a portion of his or her VA entitlement?

A: Yes. A veteran can secure any number of loans provided he has sufficient remaining entitlement.

Q: Can a Femme Sole buy VA?

A: Yes. She can obtain a VA loan if she is a veteran with remaining entitlement or the unmarried widow of a veteran who had remaining entitlement, who died in service or a service related death.

Q: Can you charge more for a house than the CRV amount?

A: Yes. The veteran must be informed of he difference, sign a statement to that effect and pay the difference as a down payment. The maximum VA amount is limited to CRV.

Q: Is there a prepayment penalty on VA?

A: No.

Q: Can a veteran pay more down?

A: Yes.

Q: What is a Conventional loan?

A: All loans made on residential type real estate which are not insured by the FHA or guaranteed by the VA.

Q: What is Mortgage Cancellation Insurance?

A: It is insurance that will pay the remaining balance of a loan to the lender should the mortgagor die.

Q: How long does an average Conventional loan approval take?

A: Six to eight weeks-depending upon the individual circumstances.

Q: Is a conventional buyer liable for full payment of his loan?

A: Yes.

Q: Can a conventional buyer purchase an FHA home?

A: Yes.

Q: What is the difference between FHA and Conventional home construction?

A: FHA and VA construction must comply with the MPS construction manual and local authorities' directives and are inspected to insure compliance. Conventional homes must comply only with local authorities' directives and have no required inspections, unless specified by a municipal code.

Q: What are the terms of Conventional mortgages?

A: Conventional mortgages can have terms of 15, 25, or 30 years.

Q: Can conventional loans be assumed?

A: No, for the most part, only on rare occasions have they been assumed.

Q: What determines the interest rate on Conventional loans?
A: The interest rates are determined by the prevailing market conditions.

Q: Is mortgage insurance required with 20% or more downpayment on a Conventional loan.
A: No.

Q: Do lenders prefer Conventional loans?
A: Generally speaking yes, because the Conventional loan requires more flexibility in the special agreements and terms of the loan and the Conventional loan avoids the profusion of paperwork typically associated with federally insured or guaranteed loans.

Experience has taught me that most people learn about finance through trial and error. Trial and error is the most expensive way to learn. There is no room in anyone's budget for costly mistakes. Buying a home can be made uncomplicated if we have a logical comprehension of finance. The above questions have been the most often asked by home buyers. Asking questions and getting the right answers, is the least expensive cost to pay for a home.

Chapter Seven

The Contract

The "Contract or Earnest Money Agreement" can unnecessarily be a source of grief and fear. Most people enter into a contract with all defenses up. What creates the defenses? It is the fear of not being able to understand entirely what one is signing. The truth of the matter is, that most people really don't completely understand what they are signing. Legal lingo can sound one way and mean another. This is the grief of a contract. I will attempt to walk you through the contract procedure. I am going to give you the basics of most new home sale's contract(s). Every builder will have his own new home contract form(s) prepared by an attorney, according to the real estate laws of that state. The contract form(s) that you will use, depends upon the type of financing that you have decided upon.

FHA, VA, Conventional and Cash, all have their own appropriate designated contract form. However, the primary requirements on all contracts are the same.

When you are ready to meet with the sales person to write a contract, please take the time to call the sales person before you go. Ask; what is the most convenient time to meet to write a contract?; and verify the availability of the home that you have selected. It could be that the property that you are wanting' is already sold. By knowing your intentions, the salesperson can protect the sale of your home before you arrive.

Protect yourself first. Make the call before you leave your home. If you are working with a Realtor, notify them of your decision and ask them to pick you up or to meet you at the sales office.

The scenario from this point, upon arrival at the sales office, is exciting. Everything is done to make you feel comfortable. If necessary ask the sales person to take you back to look at the property just one more time. When you return, ask the sales person to review the financing options and to give you an approximate total move-in cost. It is necessary to update your previous numbers in the event that financing has changed since your last discussion on finance.

I Now is the time to ask questions! Don't assume any answer. Ask! Don't precede any further until you reasonably understand the answer. Once understood, go to the next question. If you have any questions on builder negotiations, this is the time to discuss it. Not every builder will negotiate a sales price or have some giveaways to the buyer up his sleeve. Complete your question and answer session with the sales person.

Once you have accepted or understand the answers to your questions, it is time for the sales person to write the contract based upon the type of financing that you have decided upon. Ask the sales person if you might have a blank copy to read along with them as they are filing in the blanks on the original contract to be submitted. Every sales person has their own method of reading contracts. I personally, would read every word to my buyers so that they had a complete understanding of what they were signing. That is not the routine of some sales people. It does not mean that they are hiding anything from you, but that they have an understanding of the contract and can explain a contract per paragraph. If it makes you feel more comfortable, ask the sales person to read all of the contract to you instead of explaining each paragraph in a paraphrase. Why? You need to understand to the best of your knowledge, what you are about to sign.

The primary format for all contracts are the following:
The seller's name
Name or names of the purchasers of the property
Legal description of the property and property address
Purchase price
Down Payment Loan amount Type of financing (FHA, VA, Conventional, Cash) Interest rate and type (2-1 buydown, adjustable rate or fixed)
Number of years for financing (15 years or 30 years, etc.)
Number of days to obtain financing
Number of days to obtain approval
The appraisal clause
Special Provisions
Title policy
Construction terms
Selections and Improvements
Earnest Money
Closing information
Purchaser's sales expenses
Default by seller and buyer
Warranty agreements (if provided)
Possession of property
Remedies/termination of contract
Fees to the Realtor (this clause is sometimes a separate contract)
Mortgage Insurance

Builders points paid and other expenses if applicable Qualified description of the house plan
Contract date
Contract Acceptance date
Signature(s) of purchaser(s)
Signature of builder

There are a few variables on the above listed contract format, but all should contain most of the described content.

I am not an attorney representing every state in the nation and every builder in the nation. Nonetheless, I still feel confident representing the basics of a new home sale contract.

The verbiage in a contract also depends on whether or not the builder has to build you a home from the start or if you are buying a home that is a part of his standing inventory (spec house).

Another consideration would be if the builder has to wait for you to sell your home, in order for you to have the funds to close on the new home. This is called a "Contingency Sale". Not all builders can or will accept a contract on the premise that you have to sell your home before you can close on one of his homes. This is an independent decision based on a case by case situation made by the builder. Check with the sales person in regard to the builders policy on a contingency sale.

As a rule, attached to the contract are other addendums and forms that pertain to your specific needs and the builders requirements. There is always plenty of paperwork for everyone.

Once the sales person has competently completed the appropriate contract with you, you should understand what you have just signed. You should know the terms and conditions of buying a new home. You have asked questions and they were answered. To some degree, you know what to expect. The "Contract", no longer seems like the villain that you once anticipated it to be.

The sales person will then discuss your itinerary of things to do prior to closing. They are: scheduling loan application, making loan application, making all necessary selections for your home, clarifying the buyer walk through and acceptance of the home before closing.

The only thing remaining to do, is to write out a check for the earnest money required by the builder. Checks are customarily made out to the title company where the builder is purchasing the title policy.

Remember to consummate the sale, the builder has to accept and sign the contract before a sales transaction is complete. Don't assume that the builder will automatically accept your contract. If you are really serious in buying a new home, don't play games with contracts with ridiculous offers that would insult the builder.

When the contract has been accepted by the builder, you are on your way to becoming a part of the great American dream, "Homeownership".

Tomorrow you will meet with the loan officer for your loan application.

Chapter Eight

The Loan Application

"Can I or can I not use my own mortgage company to obtain a loan"? That is the question that most prospective home buyers ask. The answer depends upon the type of finance being offered or what lender is financing the construction loans.

If the builder is paying a certain number of points on any type of financing that you qualify for, then it would make little difference where you obtained your mortgage. In the event that the builder has paid a huge sum of money to purchase a commitment from a lender or is obligated to a lender through his/her construction loans, then your best opportunity would be to obtain a mortgage from that lender. Earlier on, I mentioned that, commitment money usually has the best interest rate available in the market place.

Some national home builders even have their own mortgage companies. These companies, offer excellent interest rates.

It is very difficult to compete with a national home builder who has their own mortgage company. After all, it is more difficult to sell new homes if financing is always a problem to the new home buyer. So the builder, just went one step further, and bought his own mortgage company. Of course, these mortgage companies are legitimate, and comply with state and federal guidelines.

Let's assume that at this point, you have decided upon a lender and you have already made an appointment with a loan officer. Before your appointment, there are a few essential documentations that you must collect to take with you. The following is a general list of required items that are needed for a loan application. The items will vary with a self employed person. Your loan officer will give you the detailed information that fits your situation.

Information Needed at Loan Application:

1. Social Security Number(s)
2. Residence Addresses, Include Landlord Names and Addresses for the past two years.
3. Names and Addresses of each employer(s) for the last two years.
4. Gross Monthly Salary (Current Paycheck Stubs).
5. Names, Addresses, Account Numbers & Balances of all Checking and Savings Accounts.
6. Names, Addresses, Account Numbers and Balances and Monthly Payments on all open loans.
7. Addresses of other real estate owned.

8. Loan information on other real estate owned.

9. Estimated Value of Furniture and Personal Property.

10. Certificate of Eligibility or DD214's (VA only).

11. Money for Credit Report and Appraisal (This amount is disclosed before loan application).

12. If Self-Employed—See your Loan Officer for Requirements.

13. W 2's past 2 Years and Copies of Last 2 Years Income tax returns.

14. Recorded Copies of Divorce Decrees (if applicable).

15. Copy of Earnest Money Agreement.

Your first reaction will be, "I'll never get all of this together". Believe me, it's not as impossible as it appears.

There always is additional information requested by the lender. The requested information is usually based upon the data received from your credit report such as a slow payment(s) on a debt(s), and or unexplained debts not previously reported to the loan officer.

Some people become offended by the demand of paperwork required from a lender to process a loan. As difficult as it may be, do your best to comply. No body is picking on you. You are a file that has to be processed accurately according to your lender's guidelines in the event that your loan is audited by regulators or is sold to another investor. Think of it this way, the lender is investing thousands and thousands of dollars in you and he doesn't even know you. This assembling of information tells the lender who you are and why he should lend you thousands and thousands of dollars. That's fair.

Collect together what you can before you meet with the loan officer. Bring the balance of the requested items to the loan officer in as soon as possible. A loan cannot be processed or approved without all of the necessary information requested.

Before application is made, your loan officer will review the loan application process and the financing options to you based upon your accepted contract with the builder. The loan officer then fills out a standard loan application form and other lender required forms. After completing and signing all required forms, the loan officer can more or less review your file based upon the documentation presented. At that point, he or she can only give you a personal opinion of your file. Do not take the loan officer's personal opinion as an approval or disapproval on your home loan. It is too soon to determine an outcome on your loan.

The loan officer will requalify you on your financing (payment and debt versus gross monthly income) and present you with a Good Faith Estimate, (that is an ESTIMATED total closing cost sheet). Your final closing cost cannot be determined until a closing date has been set because of interim interest, taxes, insurance and other non-predetermined cost. IT IS ONLY AN ESTIMATE.

You now wait for: the verifications of employment, loans, residence, banking, credit cards, and any lender required verification to be mailed out and to be sent back to the lender to confirm. The lender will send off for your credit report and everyone waits for the results, like a biopsy in a doctor's office.

When your credit report comes back to the lender from the credit bureau, the lender will determine it's classification. If the credit report looks good, the lender will proceed with the loan processing and order an appraisal, survey and other procedures required to document a loan. If your credit report is questionable, the lender then will make a judgment call if it is necessary to continue the loan process. Even a questionable credit report can be conquered with a proper letter of explanation accepted by the lender.

When all of the compiled information, "looks good", according to the guidelines of the lender, the file is then submitted to a committee for approval or to an underwriter for approval. Depending upon the type of loan (Conventional) the loan has to be submitted to a private mortgage insurance company if you have less than a twenty percent down payment on your loan for approval.

The amount Of time it takes to process a loan, depends upon the amount of paperwork that you have, that the processor has to mail out and document.

There are no two loans alike. The time that it takes to accurately process a loan is liked to being an attorney gathering valuable information to make his client look good to the jury. The same applies in lending. You have got to look good to the loan committee or to an underwriter to get a loan approved. Your goal and your loan officer's goal is to get you approved.

Loan approval can take one day or one week. It all depends upon the lender's policy. Sometimes you have to wait and wait for approval, by this time your are standing on your head. Even though, it's obvious that you have a good file, the anticipation of the outcome still leaves one with anxiety. That's normal. If it makes you feel any better, every one including the sales person, the builder and your loan officer are all standing on their heads. That's normal too. Everyone is routing for you. You are the reason that they are working.

You're approved, now what?

The next step will be to complete your home for move in or to start your home from ground up, depending upon the type of purchase. Now that you are an approved buyer, the builder is motivated to get you into your home as soon as possible under the terms of your contact.

The next to the last phase will be the sight inspection of your home for acceptance so that the lender can prepare the documents for your closing. This could be three days plus or minus before the actual closing. Your lender at this time, should be able to give you a more accurate account of your cash needed that you will have to bring to closing.

Chapter Nine

The Closing

The day or two before a closing is like the final rush before a wedding, to make sure that everything on your list has been completed and all arrangements are appropriately in order. Like a marriage, buying a home is a commitment. The closing, compared to a wedding, is the ceremony prior to ownership.

Before the closing, as a rule, builders allow the home buyer an opportunity to inspect their future home. The inspection is sometimes called a "Buyer Walk". Every builder has their own policy as to who will walk with the buyer during the inspection. Some builders permit the superintendent of construction, the sales person or both. The fewer the people walking the house, the easier the task. This is not a time for relatives and Realtors to exercise their competence in construction. This is a time only for the home buyer and the builder. There should be no distractions from anyone else. Keep the walk simple and to the point.

The superintendent has a check list that is long and detailed because a home cannot close until it is 100% complete. I have seen a few exceptions to the rule but the corrections have only been cosmetic not structural. Below is a summary of what a check list will most likely include. This is only a summary not an official guideline or form used in all construction. The actual form would be more accurate and detailed according to the builder's inspection policy.

Builder and Buyer Checklist:

1. EXTERIOR FRONT; Walk flatwork, Walk grass, Walk cornice, Check brick and slab, Inspect garage door, Check windows, Check front door, Check Paint.

2. RIGHT SIDE OF HOUSE; Walk grade, Check windows, Check cornice, Check brick, Check hot water pop off, Check hose bib, Check gas conduit, Check dryer vent.

3. BACK OF HOUSE; Check grade, Check flatwork, Check fence, Check soffit, Check siding, Check paint, Check windows, Check breaker box, Check light fixture, Check air conditioner condenser, Check roof.

4. FRONT LEFT OF HOUSE; Check soffit, Check windows, Check paint, Check slab, Check roof, Check brick,

5. ENTRY (EXTERIOR); Check light fixture, Check for paint and caulking, Check step, Check door bell.

6. INTERIOR ENTRY; Check mechanical, Check outlets, Check doors, Check enamel, Check latex, Check vinyl or tile.

7. KITCHEN; Check mechanical (lights, outlets, cabinets, drawers, hardware, air conditioning duct and door bumpers), Check ice

maker outlet, sink, stove, oven, microwave, All warranty books in drawer, Check dishwasher, Check windows, Check kitchen tops, Check pantry, Check enamel, Check wallpaper, Check vinyl or tile.

8. DINING ROOM; Check mechanical Check enamel, Check latex, Check carpet, Check wallpaper.

9. FAMILY ROOM; Check mechanical, Check enamel, Check, latex, Check carpet.

10. HALL; Check mechanical, Check enamel, Check latex, Check carpet.

11. MASTER BEDROOM; Check mechanical, Check enamel, Check latex, Check carpet.

12. MASTER BATH; Check mechanical, Check mirror(s), Check sinks, Check vanity, Check commode, Check ceramic tile, Check tub and fixtures, Check enamel, Check wallpaper, Check vinyl or tile.

13. ALL OTHER BEDROOMS; Check mechanical, Check enamel, Check latex, Check carpet.

14. ALL OTHER BATHROOMS; Check mechanical, Check mirror(s), Check sinks, Check vanity, Check commode, Check ceramic tile, Check tub, Check shower, Check Enamel, Check wallpaper, Check vinyl or tile.

15. GARAGE; Check mechanical, Check latex, Check floor.

16. UTILITY ROOM; Check mechanical, Check latex, Check enamel, Check vinyl or tile, Check wash and dryer connections.

17. CHECK HOT WATER HEATER

18. CHECK ALL PLUMBING

19. CHECK HEATING SYSTEM

20. CHECK COOLING SYSTEM

The check list could be endless, depending upon the style of home that you have purchased and the extra's that you have had installed.

Now that your home has been completed, the builder is now ready to set up an appointment for a walk through.

The appointed time has arrived and you are standing at the front door of your future home. The builder has his list prepared and off you go through your home. During the course of the walk through, lets say that you found a couple of unsatisfactory completion items. The builder will then discuss the items that you are in conflict over and how it can be solved and agreed upon by both parties satisfactorily. Notation on the buyers check list is made to take care of the situation. The procedure continues until you are completed with all listed items on the walk-through list. Hopefully, both parties are in agreement with the outcome of the walk-through.

In an hour or two you will have completed the walk through. Both builder and buyer has agreed in writing, along with signatures from both parties that the home has been accepted as is or that the home has been accepted with the noted corrections.

Builders will require that the home buyer come back once the corrections have been made. The buyer must totally satisfy himself or herself with the repairs so that they can accept the house in writing, before a closing can take place.

When I say, "totally accept the home", I don't mean to imply that the home is absolutely 100% perfect in every dimension of construction. A 100% PERFECT home does not exist. A 100% structurally sound home does exist. To build a structurally sound home according to the plans and specifications of the builder according to the terms of the contract is the builder's objective.

Not only do you have to accept your home, but depending upon the type of financing, the lender and its inspectors have to accept your home. Without the acceptance documents at closing, some lenders will not allow a new home to close. Think about it. Would you fund money to a company who's homes were incomplete, that could possibly create problems for the buyer? The buyer could say," I don't want this mess". Of course not. That is the purpose of the walk through and it's final acceptance by the buyer and by the lender. You must be satisfied with your new home.

Builders are aware and familiar with building acceptance policies and try to meet those standards during construction.

Inspectors come out during construction and after construction to make sure that the building codes and standards have been met.

After the acceptance by you of your home, a time will be set up for your closing. A closing can take place at a title company, a law office, or the builders office.

When the date and time has been confirmed for your closing, your loan officer or the title company (ask your sales person who will notify you) will inform you of the amount of money that you will need to bring to closing. That dollar amount is to be brought to the closing in certified funds or cash. No checks please. Customarily, this is the time to contact your insurance company regarding your homeowner's insurance and have your insurance company make arrangements to have your policy at the closing. The lender will notify you of any other compliance that you need to take care of. If in doubt, call your loan officer and ask.

If you are working with a Realtor, the Realtor will have already assisted you with some of the final preparations and expectations for closing. The Realtor will usually attend the closing with you. Your sales person, who also has helped you along the way, **will** normally not attend the closing. At closing there may be a builder representative, yourself and the person performing the closing transaction, known as "The Closer".

The date and time for your closing has finally arrived. You have been made comfortable in an office. The Closer, enters the room, introduces herself or himself and the procedure begins.

The Closer will begin by giving you a "Settlement Statement". A settlement statement is an itemized accounting of all funds involved in the sale and closing of a home. You will be asked to read it carefully, before the

Closer reads the settlement statement line by line with you. This is the time to ask questions, if you do not understand what you are paying for.

Settlement statements are easy to read and are very self explanatory. Sometimes, one just needs a moment to familiarize themselves with the unaccustomed paperwork, to understand what they are reading.

When the settlement statement has been read an understood, it is then the time for the Closer to proceed and document the balance of the lender required paperwork such as the deed, the title policy, the escrow accounts, the disclosures and various essential forms for your signature.

The Closer will interpret each document to you before you sign it. If the Closer was required to read every line on every page, unlike your sales contract, it would literally take hours and hours and hours to read.

The Closer's translation is thorough and complete. If you still don't understand, of course, ask until you do understand, what you are signing. The Closer is trained to understand, to read and to translate all legal documents from the lender and the attorneys who prepared them and to see to it that your file of paperwork is completed according to the lenders requirements. The Closer will also see to it that all of the proper documents are filed and recorded, according to the laws of your state. You will receive a copy of the entire paper transaction, customarily before leaving the closing.

The last "i" has been dotted and the last "t" has been crossed. May we now pronounce you, "home owner". You may now kiss the deed.

The sales person will be waiting at the sales office to present your keys to you. House keys are never given to the home buyer prior to closing in the event that something went wrong and the title could not be passed from the builder's name to the new home owner's name. It is the builder's house until all of the closing papers are signed.

It's time to tell the movers to start their engines. It is time to move.

All of your friends and relatives who have stood by you, during your ordeal, probably will have you packed and ready to move by the time you get back home.

There is an excitement that is unexplainable, when someone moves into a new home. Everyone is happy and everyone is ready to move.

Chapter Ten

Welcome Home

There is no joy and or excitement in the world like picking up your new home keys. It seems to make everything official. You have arrived. You have passed all of the test of endurance and you have crossed the finish line. This moment is yours.

Be sure that you have had all utilities transferred into your name at your new address as of this date. Remember also, to take care of having your mail transferred to the new address. The Post Office will furnish you with change of address cards.

It will not be long before the moving van arrives along with all of your friends in trucks loaded down with your possessions.

Once you drive up into your driveway, get out of your car, walk up to your front door and insert your key to open the front door, do you actually realize that homeownership is yours. This is what you have worked so hard for. The best is yet to come through years of home enjoyment.

Congratulations and Welcome Home!

Chapter Eleven

Construction Terminology

Everybody wants and should know construction terms. Knowing construction terms will help you understand the building progress of your home. Knowing construction terms will also allow you to discuss your home with the builder. Regardless of the price or size of your home, the terminology is still the same. Listed below, is an A-Z dictionary of terms.

ASP-9—FHA set of guidelines for development with which a builder must comply in order for the buyer to receive FHA or VA financing.

BACKFILL—The replacement of excavated earth.

BAFFEL—A piece of material, usually serrated cardboard, that is placed in an opening to hold back insulation and to allow circulation, especially between the rafters and batting.

BARGE RAFTER—Two 2" x 4"s tied together with a I" x 4" to create a 6" overhang on the gable end of a structure.

BASEBOARD—A trim piece placed against the wall around a room next to the floor to provide proper finish between floor and sheetrock.

BATT—A sheet of insulation installed between frame members.

BATTEN—Narrow strips of wood or metal used to cover joints.

BATTER BOARD—Board set on a lot to string for proper location and square angles for foundation forms. A fastening for stretched strings to indicate the outlines of foundation walls.

BAY WINDOW—Any window space projecting outward from the walls, either square or polygonal, that has shape and support in the foundation.

BEAM—A structural member transversely supporting a load.

BEE HOLES—Air space in the mortar between bricks caused by the space not being filled completely.

BEDDING—The second coat of the sheetrock finish.

BIRDSMOUTH—The portion if a rafter that is notched out to fit over the top plate of the wall.

BLACK JOINT—A material used between where flatwork is poured against existing concrete.

BLIND NAILING—Nailing in such a way that nailheads are not visible on face of work.

BLOCKING (or NAILERS)—Lumber added to the frame to give additional support to material that will later be hung to cover the frame.

BOTTOM PLATE—(also called SOLE PLATE OR TOP PLATE) The horizontal 2' x 4" piece of specially treated lumber placed at bottom of stud wall, which forms the bottom support of a frame.

BOX FRAME—A frame that is built on the ground and then Stood up and placed on foundation.

BOXWINDOW—A window that projects outward from the wall, but is not Supported by foundation, but rather overhangs it.

BRICK TIES—Galvanized steel ties about 6"—8" in length and I" in width that are nailed to studs and then bent to an "L" shape to be placed and mortared between brick to give support to the brick wall.

BULL FLOAT—A long handled hand tool with a large base used for smoothing newly placed concrete. (Also can be used as a verb).

CASING—Wide moulding used to trim door or window openings.

CAT HEADS—Steel clamps used during foundation make-up to secure cables to the form.

CAULK—A plastic or rubber based substance used to close and seal cracks to exclude water and air.

CHAIR—Plastic seats that are placed under foundation cables to make certain that concrete will flow under the cable to hold it in place.

CLEAT STOCK—A piece of lumber (usually I" x 6" or I" x 2") that is attached to closet walls to support shelving.

COLLAR TIE L—(**or COLLAR BEAM or TIE BEAM**) A horizontal piece connecting a pair of rafters, forming a strong triangle that ties the roof together so it cannot spread out.

CONSTRUCTION JOINT—2" x 611 piece of lumber placed between the main foundation of a wing wall to allow for expansion.

CORNER BEAD—The metal strip placed on corners where sheetrock meets sheetrock in order to form a straight, strong edge.

CORNICE—Exterior trim work that encloses the meeting of roof and along the eave of a structure; all exterior wood work.

CRIPPLER—Short, vertical studding placed above the garage door opening.

CROWN—The high part of bowed lumber. The crown of the lumber is always placed up or out.

DADO—To have been cut with a groove.

DEAD END—End of foundation cables that has plates with cables permanently attached.

DEADWOOD—A pieces of lumber that carries no weight and is attached to frame for hanging sheetrock, cornice, or cabinets. it is not bearing, but is instead used for nailing.

DOG EARS—Shingles that are not cut properly and stick out incorrectly.

DOWNSPOUT—A pipe for carrying rainwater down from roof gutters.

DUSTING—Process used by painter to correct overspray; the improper procedure of sprinkling portland cement on a slab to make the concrete finish more easily and dry more quickly.

EASEMENT—A strip of land that has been designated as the area to carry main lines of underground utilities, such as telephone, water, electric, or sewer. (Never place concrete on an easement).

ELEVATION—The exterior of the house. There is a front, left, right, and rear elevation to each house.

ESCUTCHEON—A protective or ornamental shield.

EXPANSION JOINT—Vertical opening running down a brick wall that accommodates expansion and contraction of brick is filled with caulking; also the redwood strips used to separate blocks of concrete in walks or drives to prevent cracking due to expansion as a result of temperature changes.

EYEBROW—A special cornice technique that is used when vertical and horizontal cornice meets.

FACENAILING—Nailing perpendicular to surface of wood.

FACIA BOARD—A flat board used in combination with mouldings as trim at end of rafters as outer face of cornice.

FIRESTOP—A solid, tight closure of a concealed space, placed to prevent air drafts and spread of fire and smoke (usually between living area and attic space).

FLATWORK—Concrete work that does not have beams or piers, such as driveways and sidewalks.

FLOAT FORM—Portion of a form that is added to basic form to gain a different level within the slab.

FLOATING—The first application of sheetrock mud to smooth the sheetrock and cover the tape.

FLUE—The passage in a chimney through which smoke ascends.

FORMSET—Materials used in building foundation forms. (should be economy grade).

FRIEZE—A horizontal member of the cornice used for finishing trim. Both brick friezes and shingle friezes are used.

FURDOWN—Building out a wall or ceiling to even it, to.carry ducts, to form an air space, or to give wall an appearance of greater thickness.

GABLE—The vertical triangular end of a building from cornice to ridge.

GAMBREL CEILING—A ceiling that rises at an angle from all sides to a flat ceiling.

GIRDER—A large or principal beam to support secondary beams.

GLASS BEAD—Moulding used to finish joint between formica counter top in kitchen and wall or between marble vanity top and wall.

GOAT'S LEG—**(or LAMB'S LEG)**—The corner overhang of a cornice.

GRADE—The level of ground at building site.

GREENBOARD—Green sheetrock that is especially treated for water resistance. It is placed around the tub before applying ceramic tile.

GREENPLATE—Pressure treated lumber used for sole plate.

GROUND FAULT INTERRUPTER—A safety breaker in an electrical outlet (switch or plug) when installed near water.

GROUT—Mortar used to fill joints of masonry.

GYP—Asphalt impregnated sheathing, usually in 4' x 8' sheets, that is placed behind exterior brick for insulation.

HEADER—A beam placed to span an opening, such as a window or door, and constructed of two boards (2x4, 2x6, 2x8, or 2x1O), usually with a 1/2" plywood fill between.

HIP—The external roof line formed by the meeting of two sloping sides of a roof.

HOLIDAY—The absence of paint where it should be on a finished wall.

HONEYCOMB—The non-smooth outside area of concrete in a foundation caused by unsolid packing against the form.

HOSE BIB—The outside faucet.

HYDROMULCH—A mixture of Bermuda grass seed, fertilizer, and adhesive in liquid form that is pumped through a hose and sprayed over lot.

JACK RAFTER—A rafter that spans the distance from the wallplate to a hip, or from a valley to a ridge.

JAMB, DOOR—Surrounding case into which and Out of which a door closes and opens; upright pieces called jambs and head.

JITTERBUG—A tool with a long handle and a bottom plate made of steel that is perforated with many holes, 1/2" in diameter. Used on newly poured concrete to make certain that top portion is free of large solid matter such as stones.

JOIST—Any of the beams ranged parallel from wall to wall in a structure to support a floor or ceiling.

KICKER—A piece of lumber nailed at approximately a 45 degree angle against the form to hold it tightly in place.

LINTEL—A horizontal crosspiece member spanning and usually carrying the load above an opening.

LOOKOUT—The part of the cornice that ties the rafters to the side of the house and is used primarily for nailing a soffit.

MASTIC—A tacky material used as protective coating or to fill gaps.

MCRV—(Master Certificate of Reasonable Value) A value of the structure assessed by VA that is the maximum amount to be loaned on the home.

NAILERS—See blocking.

O/C OR O.C.—On center.

OVERSPRAY—Paint on improper areas caused by spray painting without the protection of shield to the affected area.

PANEL—A group of homesites that are adjacent and upon which homes are constructed simultaneously. Construction cannot begin on a panel until 80% of the homes are sold.

PERMANENT POWER—Installation of permanent residential meter to service home with electrical power.

PIGTAIL—Copper plumbing installed in slab before concrete is placed to carry water from the electrical power.

PITCH—The rise of the roof expressed in inches per foot of run.

PLASTICITY INDEX—An index used to reference the hardness or buildability of the ground.

PLENUM—The junction box above the central air conditioning unit that distributes air flow to the ducts.

PLINTH—The base support between garage doors on which center post is built.

PLUMB—Straight down or up; vertical.

POCKET FORMER—Circular plastic device placed on live end of foundation cable to form a pocket in the concrete around the cable for purpose of stressing.

POLYCELL—An insulating substance that is spread into all small openings to the outside, such as space around the window frames and holes for pipes.

PONY WALL—A wall that is added above the top plate to gain extra height and give support to rafters.

PRIMER—The first, protective coat of paint.

PUNCH OUT—To check off a stage of construction to make certain that all things have been completed to standard.

PURLIN—A horizontal framing piece that supports the rafters of a roof.

PURLIN BRACES—Vertical framing pieces that support the purlin.

QUOINS—Brick projections on a corner of a house that are added for decoration.

RAFTER TAIL—The end of a rafter that extends beyond main walls of structure.

RAT RUN—Board run above the ends of ceiling joist to keep them straight and unmoving.

REBAR—Steel reinforcing rod used in concrete walls and footings.

REGISTER—Devise for releasing air flow from heating or air conditioning unit.

REGISTER BOX—The outlet where air emerges from the heating and air conditioning ducts. During the trim stage, it will be covered with a movable grill that can direct the flow of air.

RIDGE BOARD—The board placed on edge at top of roof to support upper ends of rafters.

ROOF JACK—Fitting place around roof pipe to prevent leakage and hold pipe in place.

ROWLOK—A brick ledge or sill.

SADDLE—Part of door frame.

SCREED—Part of a door frame.

SHIM SHINGLE—Wooden roofing materials that are ordered to be used to tighten space around door frame.

SILL PLATE—The bottom of a door or window.

SISIE—Abbreviation for I smooth side, I smooth edge.

SKIMMING—The final coat of sheetrock mud applied after floating in order to give a smooth finish.

SOFFIT—The under side, especially in a cornice.

SOLDIER COURSE—A row of vertical bricks used at top of brick wall for finishing. (A walking soldier course has every other brick protruding at a slight angle).

SOLE PLATE—See Bottom Plate.

SPLASH BLOCK—A concrete block placed under a gutter downspout to avoid washouts where the water hits the earth.

STICK FRAME—A frame built foundation from bottom plate up.

STIPPLE—The texture put on wall board.

STOMP—A paint treatment made on ceilings with a special brush in order to create designs.

STORY POLES—2" x 4"s nailed to corners of structure as a guide to a bricklayer.

STRONGBACK—A 2" x 6" nailed to a 2" x 4" and then nailed perpendicularly above joists to keep joists in place and from bending, turning, or bowing.

STUD—One of a series of slender wood members placed as supporting elements in walls.

STUD SHOE—A support for a stud where it has been notched for plumbing.

SUMP—A pit or reservoir serving as a drain or receptacle for liquids.

SWALE—A low lying or depressed stretch of land (Created for drainage).

T-POLE—Pole to which temporary power line and meter are connected during construction. T-poles should be set to service more than one panel of homes.

TAKE-OFF—Amount of any material that is deemed to be proper amount necessary to complete job.

TENDON—The cable used in supporting foundation.

TIE BEAM—See Collar Tie.

TOENAILING—Nailing at a slant with initial surface to permit penetration into second member.

TOE PLATE—See Bottom Plate.

TOP PLATE—The horizontal continuous 2-x 4" doubled lumber along the top of a stud wall.

TRIM—The finish materials, such as mouldings and baseboards.

UNDERGROUNDS—Permanent utilities run underground.

VALLEY—A rafter that forms the intersection of an internal roof angle. The angled portion of a roof where two slopes meet.

VENEER—The outside finish, such as brick veneer or wood veneer.

WALKING SOLDIER COURSE—A row of vertical bricks where every other brick is slanted out at bottom.

WEATHERSTRIP—Any material used at doors and windows to retard passage of air, moisture and dust.

WEDGE—A heavy metal piece that is placed around a cable and inserted into the circular opening in the foundation created by the pocket former. The wedge is properly placed to aid in the process of stressing the cables.

WEEPHOLE—A space left in a brick wall near the bottom so the moisture that collects in the space between brick and gyp can escape.

WETLINE EASEMENT—An easement that carries water or sewer lines.

WINGWALL—A decorative brick wall, usually in front of house, whose weight is carried on a concrete ledge extended from the main slab.

WOLMANIZE—A Chemical process to treat wood for rot resistance. There are always questions asked, above and beyond terminology. To familiarize you further with construction, I have listed below the most frequent asked questions and the best possible answers.

Q: What is the best foundation?
A: Post-tension.

Q: What is a post-tension foundation?
A: Concrete placed over cables. After the concrete has cured, cables are stressed to approximately 28,000 p.s.i..

Q: Why does a post tension foundation develop cracks?
A: When the concrete is cured, the cables will be stressed. In the interim period, concrete will develop settling cracks due to evaporation on hot and windy days.

Q: What is a floating slab foundation?
A: Same as post-tension.

Q: What is a pier foundation?
A: Concrete footing for support of wood floor framing.

Q: What is a foundation beam?
A: Reinforced concrete footing to support building.

Q: What is the purpose for fill under a foundation?
A: Smooth bearing surface for foundation to allow for expansion and contraction.

Q: Are foundations weatherproofed for moisture?
A: Yes.

Q: What causes a foundation to sweat?
A: Condensation of atmospheric moisture.

Q: What is a composition shingle?
A: A shingle made from a composite of asphalt or fiberglass and gravel.

Q: Why are composition shingles used.?
A: They are fire retardant, less prone to roof leaks, and are the best value.

Q: What is the advantage of composition roof over wood shingles?
A: Wood shingles rot, warp, leak and burn.

Q: Why is copper wiring better than other wiring?
A: It does not build up an electrical resistance to another metal.

Q: What is the minimum insulation required by FHA?
A: R-13 in the walls, R-22 in the ceiling.

Q: What does the "R" stand for in "R-1 3"?
A: Coefficient of heat transmission. The higher the R-value the more thermal resistance you have.

Q: Is there any other forms of insulation in a home?
A: Polycell and caulk are used to seal cracks around windows and doors to insure no leakage and weatherstripping is used around all doors to prevent energy loss.

Q: What are the advantages of having steel doors?
A: Steel doors are insulated, don't warp, splinter and are harder to break into.

Q: Why are aluminum windows used?
A: They are longer lasting than wood, don't warp and require less maintenance.

Q: What does the power vent do?
A: Pulls the hot air out of the attic.

Q: What are the gaps between bricks?
A: Brick walls need to have expansion joints to accommodate expansion and contraction due to weather.

Q: What is a ridge?
A: The peak of a roof.

Q: What is a hip roof?
A: A roof that slopes away from the ridge at all angles.

Q: What is a gable roof?
A: A roof slopes away from the ridge in two directions.

Q: What is a gambrel ceiling?
A: A ceiling that rises at an angle from all sides to a flat ceiling.

Q: What is a cathedral ceiling?
A: A ceiling that meets at a peak, usually with a beam in the middle.

Q: What is a vaulted ceiling?
A: A ceiling that rises at angles from two sides to a flat ceiling.

Q: What are the advantages of a stainless steel sink?
A: No chips. Always keeps a new luster if maintained properly.

Q: What does a VA and FHA final inspection cover?
A: Everything (Inspections begin prior to slab and finish when the home is ready for occupancy).

Q: Do conventional homes have final inspections?
A: Yes, made by the lender.

Q: Does VA and FHA require gutters?
A: Yes. Gutters go over all entries and on most horizontal areas of the roof.

Q: What are the vented openings in the eave of a home?
A: Soffit vents for attic ventilation.

Q: What is the purpose of soffits?
A: Permits air flow through attic to cool it down.

You will have your own set of questions to add to this list depending upon the type of construction used by the builder. Hopefully, you have gained knowledge and understand the makeup of construction in layman's terms.

Chapter Twelve

Mortgage Terminology

Mortgage lending has its own set of foreign terms that can be confusing to the buyer. The more you know about mortgage lending, the less confusing and easier the loan process. To complete our passage through our learning experience let us now review mortgage terminology.

APPLICATION—A form used to record pertinent information on the buyer's employment, assets and liabilities to a representative of a lending institution.

APPLICATION FEE—A fee charged by the lender at application to cover the initial cost of appraisal and credit report fees.

APPRAISAL—A report made on the estimated value of property, the community's common areas and appearance, the relationship of the subject and the community.

APPRAISED VALUE—An opinion of value reached **by** an appraiser based upon knowledge, experience and a study of pertinent data.

APPRAISER—One who is approved by VA/FHA or an investor to estimate the value of real and personal property.

APPRECIATION—An increase in value, the opposite of depreciation.

BARON SOLE—A single man.

BUST OUT—A buyer who does not consummate purchase.

CASH DISCOUNT—Discount off the sales price allowed for cash payment.

CASH PURCHASE—When the property is bought without a loan.

CERTIFICATE OF ELIGIBILITY—A certificate issued by the VA to the veteran establishing eligibility to buy a home under the VA program.

CHANGE ORDER—A letter to VA or FHA requesting a change in plans or specifications, having been previously submitted and approved.

CLOSER—Person at the lending institution that prepares legal documents going to the title company.

CLOSING—The conclusion of a transaction. In real estate, closing includes the delivery of a deed, financial adjustments, the signing of a note (and the disbursement of funds necessary to the sale or loan transaction) and funding.

CLOSING COSTS—Money paid by the borrower and setter to effect the closing of a mortgage loan. This normally includes an origination fee, discount points, title insurance, survey, attorney fees including the escrow deposits for taxes, insurance and PMI.

COLD WAR LOAN—FHA loan for veterans who are eligible for full VA benefits and for veterans not eligible for full VA benefits, also referred to as an FHA 203B-Vet loan,

CO-MORTGAGORS—Two parties buying property jointly. All names CO-BORROWERS on all legal documents.

COMMITMENT FEE—Any fee paid by a potential borrower to a potential lender for the lender's promise to lend money at a specified date in the future.

COMPLIANCE INSPECTION—A report given to a lender REPORT by a designated compliance inspector **indicating** whether or not construction or repairs have complied to conditions established by a prior inspection.

CONDITIONAL COMMITMENT—A commitment by the FHA to insure an FHA loan to qualified buyer indicating a maximum loan amount value of the property and estimated closing cost.

CO-SIGNER—A second party who signs papers with an applicant on the note but not on the Deed of Trust.

CONVENTIONAL LOAN—A mortgage loan offered to those not eligible for a VA loan, and not wishing to **apply** for a FHA loan.

CREDIT RATING—A rating given a person or company to establish credit worthiness based upon present financial condition, experience and past credit
history.

CREDIT REPORT—A report to a prospective lender on the credit standing of a prospective borrower, use to help determine credit worthiness.

CRV (CERTIFICATE OF REASONABLE VALUE) A document issued by the VA establishing maximum value and loan amount for VA guaranteed mortgages and any changes to be made to the property to make it eligible for a VA guaranteed loan.

DEPOSIT—A sum of money given to bind a sale of real estate. Also known as earnest money.

DEPRECIATION—A loss of value in real property brought about by age, physical deterioration or functional or economical obsolescence. Broadly, a loss of value from any cause. The opposite of appreciation.

DISCLOSURE STATEMENT—A statement prepared by the title company that discloses all costs incurred by the buyer and seller in the transaction.

DISCOUNT POINT(S)—An amount equal to one percent of the principal amount of an investment or note. Loan discount points are a one-time charge assessed at closing by the tender to increase the yield on the mortgage loan to a competitive position with other types of investments.

DOWN PAYMENT—The difference between the sale price of real estate and the mortgage amount.

EASEMENT—Right or interest in the land of another entitling the holder to a specific limited use, privilege, or benefit such as laying a sewer, putting up electrical power lines or crossing the property.

ECOA (EQUAL CREDIT OPPORTUNITY ACT)—A federal law that requires lenders and other creditors to make credit equally available without discrimination based on race, color, sex, religion, age, marital status, or receipt of income from public assistance programs.

EFFECTIVE GROSS INCOME (PERSONAL) Normal annual income including effective that is regular or guaranteed. It may be from more than one source. Salary is generally the principal source, but other income may be significant and stable, and thus qualify.

EFFECTIVE GROSS INCOME (PROPERTY) Stabilized income that a property is expected to generate after a vacancy and bad debt allowance.

EQUITY—In real estate, the difference between fair market value and current indebtedness, usually referred to as the owner's interest.

ESCROW OFFICER/ CLOSER—Title company's representative that closes loan transactions.

ESCROW PAYMENT—That portion of a mortgagor's monthly payment held by the lender to pay off taxes, hazard insurance, mortgage insurance, lease payments and other items as they become due. Known as impounds or reserves in some states.

ET UX—And wife.

FEMME SOLE—A single woman.
FHA (FEDERAL HOUSING ADMINISTRATION) A division of the Department of Housing and Urban Development. It's main activity is the insuring of residential mortgage loans made by private lenders. It sets standards for construction and underwriting. FHA does not lend money, nor plan, nor construct housing.

FHLB (FEDERAL HOME LOAN BANK)—A regulatory and supervisory agency for federally chartered savings institution. It oversees the operations of the Savings and Loan Insurance Corp. and the Federal Home Loan Mortgage Corp.

FIRM COMMITMENT—FHA'S agreement to make a loan to a specific borrower on a specific property. An FHA or PMI agreement to insure a loan on a specific property, with a designated borrower.

FIRST MORTGAGE—A real estate loan that creates a FIRST LIEN primary lien against real property.

GIFT LETTER—A statement from the party giving funds to a 2nd. party of the amount to be given and that the 2nd. party is not liable to make repayment of the funds.

G.I. LOAN—Colloquial term given to a mortgage loan guaranteed by the VA.

GREEN CARD (ALIEN CARD)—Is given to a non U.S. citizen to verify legal residence status. Foreign Diplomats are exempt. FHA will require proof of permanent residency prior to approval. Most Conventional loans are also requiring green card verification.

GUARANTEED LOAN—A loan guaranteed by VA, the FHA or any other interested party.

HAZARD INSURANCE—A contract whereby an insurer, for a premium, undertakes to compensate the insured for loss on a specific property due to certain hazards.

HOMEOWNER'S ASSOCIATION—An organization of homeowners residing within a particular development whose major purpose is to maintain and provide community facilities and services for the common enjoyment of the residents.

HOMEOWNER'S POLICY—A multiple peril policy commonly called "package policy". It is available to owners of private dwellings and covers the dwelling and contents in the event of fire or wind damage, theft, liability or property damage, and personal liability.

HUD—The Department of Housing and Urban Development, established by the Housing and Home Finance Agency. It is also responsible for the implementation and administration of government housing and urban development programs. The broad range of programs includes community planning and development, housing production and mortgage credit (FHA), equal opportunity in housing, research and technology.

INFILE—A credit report taken from a credit bureau computer to reflect the applicants credit history. It will normally need to be updated and given to the tender in written form.

INSURED LOAN—A loan insured by FHA or a private mortgage insurance company.

INTEREST—Consideration in the form of money paid for the use of money, usually expressed as an annual percentage.

LEGAL DESCRIPTION—The recorded identification of property. Usually shown as Lot, Block, Section County and State.

LEASE AGREEMENT—A written document containing the conditions under which the possession and use of real property are given by the owner to another for a stated period and for a stated consideration.

LEVEL PAYMENT MORTGAGE/FIXED MORTGAGE—A mortgage that provides a constant fixed payment at periodic intervals during its term. Part of the payment is credited to interest with the balance of the payment used to reduce the principal.

LIEN—A legal hold or claim of one person on the property of another as security for a debt. The right given by law to satisfy debt.

LOAN AMOUNT—The loan balance after a down payment. The original principal on the note for veterans, which doesn't require a down payment.

LOAN APPROVAL, FHA APPROVAL, VA APPROVAL—The final decision made by the lending institution's underwriter or loan committee to grant an applicant a loan. This is done after all pertinent papers and documents have been prepared and submitted by the Loan Processor.

LOAN APPROVAL—A loan that has been granted WITH CONDI-TIONS subject to the applicant meeting certain terms and conditions, i.e., Proof of Sale of Prior Residence.

LOAN LETTERS—Information provided by an applicant to the lender to explain any situation which could prevent his/her quailing for a loan.

LOAN OFFICER—The lending institution representative that takes loan applications and assists customers with their loan request.

LOAN PROCESSOR—The lending institution representative that prepares pertinent papers and documents on loans for loan submission and approval. May also take loan applications and assist customers with their loan request.

LOAN SUBMISSION—A complete package of pertinent papers and documents regarding a specific borrowers) and property which is reviewed and considered by a lender for the purpose of making a mortgage loan.

LTV (LOAN TO VALUE RATIO)—The relationship between the amount of the mortgage loan and the sale price and/or appraised value whichever is lower, expressed as a percentage of the sale price and/or appraised value.

MAINTENANCE FUND—A fee by a property owner for maintenance of common grounds.

MORTGAGEE—A person or firm to whom property is conveyed as security for a loan made by such person or firm (a creditor).

MORTGAGEE'S TITLE POLICY—A title policy for the buyer, see Title Insurance Policy.

MORTGAGE INSURANCE (PREMIUM MIP)—The consideration paid by a mortgagor for insurance required by FHA.

MORTGAGOR—One who borrows money, giving as security a mortgage or deed of trust on real property (a debtor).

MORTGAGORS' TITLE POLICY—A title policy for the buyer, see Title Insurance.

NET INCOME—Effective gross income minus taxes.

ORIGINATION FEE—A fee charged for the work involved in the preparation and submission of proposed mortgage loan.

PAPERS—Legal documents prepared by the lender and sent to the Title Company for closing.

PARTIAL GUARANTEE—A VA eligibility where part of eligibility has been used.

PMI (PRIVATE MORTGAGE INSURANCE) Insurance written by a private company protecting the mortgage lender against loss occasioned by a mortgage default.

PRELIMINARY INTEREST—A daily interest charged by the lender from the funding date to the last day of the month in which the loan closes.

PREPAID ITEMS—Fees collected at closing for real estate taxes, hazard and\or homeowners insurance, MIP or PMI renewal premiums to set up escrow accounts and interest charges covering any period after the loan settlement date. It is required that the purchaser of the property pay for all prepaid items.

PREPAYMENT PENALTY—A penalty charged by a lender when a loan is prepaid or paid in full before a maturity date. This requirement has been lifted on all loans in the state of Texas.

PRINCIPAL—The loan balance that is reduced the monthly payments.

QUALIFY—Term used to indicate that an applicant has met the guidelines of the lender to be granted a loan.

RE-OPEN LOAN—To request, to reconsider a rejected loan.

REINSTATEMENT OF ELIGIBILITY—VA term meaning to re-establish for a VA loan.

REJECTED—When a loan is disapproved by the lender in preliminary underwriting, when applicants do not meet guidelines, or by VA, FHA, or Conventional investor after completely processed.

RELEASE OF LIABILITY—An agreement by a lender to terminate the personal obligation of a mortgagor in connection with the payment of a debt.

RENT REFUND—Refund of temporary rent fees paid for days not used by renter.

REQUEST FOR APPRAISAL INCREASE—Request to FHA, VA or Conventional appraiser for an increase in the property value.

RESPA (REAL ESTATE)—A federal law to provide home mortgage borrowers with information of known or estimated cost. RESPA also limits amount lenders may require to be held in an escrow account for realestate taxes and insurance, requires the disclosure of known settlement cost to both the buyers and sellers by the person conducting the settlement and outlaws certain referral fees.

SOURCE OF FUNDS—A statement from the borrower(s) to the lender of where the funds for the down payment and closing cost were obtained. If the borrower has fully earned or received the funds from a gift, they should state that none of the funds towards the purchase of the home are borrowed.

SPECIAL CLOSING—A closing time arranged outside of normal business hours.

SPECIAL HANDLING—Rushing approval of a loan.

TAXES—A fee paid for services rendered by public agencies.

TAX PRORATION—Amount of taxes paid by builder at closing.

TITLE INSURANCE POLICY—A contract by which the insurer, usually a title insurance company agrees to pay the insured a specific amount for any loss caused by defects of title to real estate, wherein the insured has an interest as purchaser, mortgagee or otherwise.

VARIABLE RATE MORTGAGE—A mortgage agreement that allows for adjustment of interest rate in keeping with a fluctuating standard. The terms pre-agreed upon in the rate.

VA (VETERANS ADMINISTRATION) – An independent agency of the federal government created in 1930. The Servicemen's Readjustment Act of 1944 authorized the agency to administer a variety of benefit programs designed-to facilitate the adjustment of returning veterans to civilian life. The VA home loan guaranty program is designed to encourage lenders to qualify eligible veterans by guaranteeing the lender against loss.

VERIFICATION OF EMPLOYMENT—Written statement of employment from buyer's employer secured by a signed form through the lender.

WARRANTY DEED—Deed to the home or legal certification of ownership.

WATER DISTRICT TAX—A tax levied by the water district.

1ST PAYMENT DATE—Date first payment will be due on the mortgage.

2 YEAR JOB REQUIREMENT—An applicant must submit a 2-year history of stable employment.

203B—Standard FHA loan program.

5% DOWN—The minimum amount required down own a Conventional loan.

30 YEAR LOAN—The normal term of an FHA, VA, and Conventional loan.

100% VA LOAN—A VA loan requiring no down payment.

DD214—A veteran's discharge and service record.

This chapter should help you relate to the chapter on finance. Go back now to Chapter Six as a referral base to capitalize on your learning of finance terminology and definition.

Chapter Thirteen

The Conclusion

This book was designed to bring you out of your house and to walk you up to the front porch of a new home. I have provided you with a documentary account of purchasing a home from the investigative beginnings to the actual events of purchasing a home, including the loan process to picking up the keys after closing.

The emotions, quiet thoughts and questions presented on the subject matter are real. Buyers really do think, feel and act as I have portrayed them. Sales people in new home sales, are thoroughly trained to discover your needs, to provide you with adequate information and to close the sale.

Purchasing a home is an emotional decision because our individual needs for a home are based on our own emotional needs. If all we ever needed was a simple covering for shelter, then it would not matter where you lived and raised a family.

The facts that I have focused on, have come from real life hands-on experiences, from home buyers. Never before have I seen so many misinformed home buyers and Realtors. This was the incentive for writing an informed new home buying book.

Today, more than ever before, there are younger home buyers buying in the higher end housing market. This upward trend of buying is a sign that the economy is getting stronger and that the buyers and the Realtors need to be prepared.

The real goal of everyone involved in a new home sales transaction is to satisfy the buyer's needs to the best of everyone's ability in relationship to what the market and builder can handle at that given time.

There is no absolute perfect builder, sales person, Realtor, new home or new home buyer. Still, if given the real simple facts and everyone is participating in a spirit of accord to make things happen, buying a new home can be the event of a life time.

The housing industry can be a tough and unpredictable market place. In spite of this, there are many things that remain the same. "**The Official Guide to New Home Buying**" is, in the simplest layman's terms, an actual profile of the basic formula for buying a new home.

I wish you the best in your home search and by the way, **Happy Home Hunting!**